LIBERIA TO THE UNITED STATES

STATES

A Liberian Girl Life Journey
"Coming To America"
An Autobiography

GWENDOLYN P. CASSELL
AUSTIN-COLLINS

Published And Distributed By
Pointe of View Intl. Inc. Publishing House
Los Angeles, California
Email: gwenpcaustin@gmail.com

Packaging/Consulting
Professional Publishing House
1425 W. Manchester Ave. Ste B
Los Angeles, California 90047
323-750-3592
Email: professionalpublishinghouse@yahoo.com
www.Professionalpublishinghouse.com

Cover design: TWA Solutions
First printing April 2024
ISBN: 979-8-218-40629-5
10987654321

Dedication

I am dedicating this book to my parents. My father, James David Cassell, Sr. and my mother, Marie Augusta Coleman-Cassell. Who were the best parents in the world to me and my siblings. They taught me everything I know from my childhood to adulthood. They taught me to be strong. My father always told me to get a good education because no one can ever take it away from me. To never let anybody take advantage of me, to always stand for what is right and to believe in myself.

I am also dedicating my book to dearest aunty Florence Eleanor Coleman-Hunter, who I will keep in my heart forever. She took me in her home with open arms after I had no place to go, when I had to leave Langston University, Langston, OK, at the end of my first semester because I had no money to pay my second semester tuition. I don't know where I would be today If she hadn't taken me in her home. To me, she was an Angel sent from God to save me when I needed her the most at that moment.

TABLE OF CONTENTS

INTRODUCTION

I wanted to tell my story because I felt it could inspire a young person who traveled thousands of miles alone, crossing oceans, leaving their family behind, and looking for a better life. No matter where they come from or where they're going, they could, in some small way, relate to my story.

As an immigrant who came to this country alone with nothing but hopes and dreams and a few dollars in my pocket, I embarked on a journey that required hard work, determination, and perseverance to achieve success. Looking back over the many years I have lived and worked in this great country, the USA, and reflecting on how much I have been able to accomplish, I realize it took a lot of guts, determination, and resilience. I always felt that I had a strong desire somewhere in my mind to succeed in life, and failure was never an option.

On the day I boarded that plane alone, leaving my family, especially my mother, grandmother, and younger siblings behind, to travel far away to the unknown, I told my nineteen-year-old self that I was going to be all right. I also knew I couldn't depend on anybody except God and myself to survive this adventure I was about to embark on. Even though at that moment, I was afraid of the uncertainty, somehow I felt hopeful about my future in America.

My childhood dream of coming to America was about to become a reality for me. I always felt deep down in my heart that if I ever made it to America, I would never forget my family and where I came from, especially my mother, who had sacrificed so much for her family. They meant the world to me, and I wanted them to be proud.

My mother was a young widow with eight children, three adults, and five minors living at home and depending on her for support. As the oldest girl and the third child of eight siblings, I always felt like a second mother to my younger siblings. After graduating from high school and leaving home at nineteen, I felt a strong sense of responsibility to my family, especially after losing our father at the young age of fifty-two to a massive heart attack.

A housewife/homemaker for twenty-four years of marriage to our father, my mother suddenly became a widow and the sole provider for her family at age forty-two. She had no choice but to get a job to support her family. I was determined to help her as soon as I could. My plan was to get a job during the day and attend college at night to earn enough money to support myself and send money to her in Liberia to help with my younger siblings.

Blessed and fortunate to get a job in banking, I worked during the day and attended college at night for four years until I graduated with a B.A. Degree in Business Administration. Living, learning, and working in America allowed me to take advantage of the many opportunities available to me as an immigrant.

I purchased my first brand-new car, a Chevy Vega, with the help of a good friend in 1973, after moving to Los Angeles in September 1970. Living and working in Los Angeles in the seventies also allowed me to help two of my brothers, Delano and John, who were still in Liberia and desperately wanted to come to America for a better life.

They had no money nor the means to raise the money they needed to purchase their tickets. I purchased their tickets on credit with a Pan American Airlines credit card, which they paid back as soon as they both got jobs. Upon arriving in Los Angeles, they lived with me in my small apartment until they got their own place.

My youngest brother, John, moved to Houston, Texas, after living in Los Angeles for a few years. My second brother, Delano, stayed in Los Angeles and started his own business: Cassell and Cassell Messenger and Delivery Service. Two of my younger sisters, Mai and Sophrinia, who I encouraged to move to Los Angeles since I always wanted to be close to my family, lived with me in a small two-bedroom duplex in South Central Los Angeles for several years.

Sophrinia graduated from Manual Arts High School in 1976. She also graduated from the Southern California Institute of Architecture Science in 1981 with a degree in Architecture. Mai got married, moved out, and started a family of her own.

I was one of the first in my immediate family, except for my older brother, James, who traveled to America and eventually to Los Angeles, where I made it my home. I fell in love with the City of Angels the moment I arrived in Los Angeles. Leaving the airport, riding down Century Boulevard, I couldn't help but notice how clean and beautiful the city and streets were, lined with tall palm trees on both sides, reminiscent of a picture-perfect tropical island seen in magazines.

As an adult, I always kept a close connection with my family, especially my siblings and their children, my nieces and nephews. Family always meant a lot to me, and it felt better and stronger after I started a family of my own. Thanksgiving became my favorite holiday of the year, and I wanted to spend it with my entire family and friends.

Growing up in Liberia, my parents always celebrated Thanksgiving dinner at our home with turkey and all the trimmings, inviting family and friends over. I enjoyed helping my mother cook and serve the food, playing games like Scrabble, cards, and checkers. Keeping up with our family traditions was very important and meant a lot to me.

After I moved to America and started a family of my own, with a home large enough to bring everyone together on Thanksgiving, my husband and I hosted Thanksgiving dinner at our home every year. I was very grateful and thankful to be in the position to host my family for Thanksgiving dinner in Los Angeles for many years.

It felt good, inside and out, spending this special day with family, especially my mom and close friends, being thankful and sharing the turkey with all the trimmings we enjoyed cooking. After dinner, we enjoyed playing games like Taboo and card games.

CHAPTER I

My Birth—The Beginning

I was born in Monrovia, Liberia, a tiny country on the West Coast of Africa. According to my parents, I came into this world when my mother was on her way to the hospital, delivering me in a pickup truck. She told me my father was very anxious and confused when she informed him she was in labor and needed to go to the hospital right away. It took him some time to gather himself and arrange a family friend's pickup to take her to the hospital. On their way, I came into this world in the pickup truck and was occasionally called the "pickup baby." I was the third child and the first girl born to my parents, with two older brothers and five younger siblings.

On the West Coast of Africa, Liberia is a small country bordered by the Atlantic Ocean to the south and west, Sierra Leone to the northwest, Ivory Coast/Cote d'Ivoire to the east, and Guinea to the north. The population is approximately 4.9 to five million people, and Monrovia, the capital, has a population of nine hundred thousand to one million.

Before delving further into my story, it's essential to highlight the early history of Liberia and its formation.

THE REPUBLIC OF LIBERIA

"If Liberia has failed, then, it is no evidence of failure of the Negro in government. It is merely evidence of the failure of slavery."
– Carter G. Wooden

In 1824, the original settlement on Cape Mesurado, which had by then somewhat expanded, was named Monrovia after President James Monroe. The combined colonies in the territory came to be known as Liberia, celebrating liberty. By the 1830s, much of the shocking early attrition had begun to ease, and with improvements in medicine and sanitation, the foundations of a modern settlement began to take hold. Although the territory remained governed by the American Colonization Society and American government officials, as it matured, it began to enjoy more comprehensive self-government.

In those early days, expansion did not penetrate deep into the interior, and it would not be until the turn of the 20th century that the boundaries of the nations were finally established. The interior landscape was heavily forested and populated by largely hostile tribes, always presenting a forbidding prospect. Coastal settlements proliferated; however, with Monrovia leading the development of the main ports of Robertport and Buchanan, and smaller settlements like Sasstown and Grand Cess developing their own individual trade networks with the interior.

In 1818, the principal colonies united to form the Commonwealth of Liberia. Additional colonies joined the union in 1842, and by the dawn of the 1840s, the first black Governor of the colony, Joseph Jenkins Roberts, had taken up the position.

Most of the emerging administration and civil service consisted of black members, and the colony was effectively operating as an independent entity. Even as the colony expanded and governed itself, it remained constantly bankrupt. Weary of the financial burden of supporting it, the federal government of the American Colonization Society urged Governor Roberts to declare the colony independent.

In 1847, this was done, and the colony duly became the independent Republic of Liberia. A constitution, along the lines of the United States Constitution, was drafted, and Joseph Jenkins Roberts became the first president. Over the next 40 years, about 19,000 African-American repatriates, sometimes known as Americo-Liberians, settled in Liberia, alongside 5,000 or more African recaptives and a handful of West Indian immigrants.

Initially, the Republic of Maryland remained separate from Liberia, with its capital and harbor situated a few miles west of the current international frontier with Cote d'Ivoire. Eventually, it merged with Greater Liberia in 1857, leaving Maryland as just an administrative division alongside many others. At the establishment of the republic, there existed no democratic frontiers, but only hazily defined eastern and western borders and a very ill-defined hinterland.

The civilization of the main centers extended no more than a few miles inland, beyond which the country was primal, heavily forested, and unexplored. The three main indigenous groups were Gola, Mel, and Kru, alongside 16 separate ethnic groups. In general, the native population was animist (although there was some Islamic influence in the north) and often extremely primitive in lifestyles and highly superstitious. Conversely, the 5,000 or so surviving immigrants from the U.S. who settled prior to 1847 had no previous exposure to animist beliefs and traditional lifestyles, being, in general, Christian and heirs to the shared memories of an entirely different culture.

They sought to recreate the culture on Liberian soil, promoting Protestant Christianity, the English language, and the construction of buildings and towns based on the southern pattern. They dressed in an exaggerated reflection of the high societies of the time, and they cultivated manners reflecting the society of the Antebellum South. Naturally, they dominated government, trade, and the professions, and they were relatively educated and comparatively wealthy. In some instances, they were very wealthy indeed.

On the other side of the coin, the indigenous locals were deliberately marginalized, existing in a parallel society with very few of the benefits of the modern society on their soil. The Americo-Liberians, as they came increasingly to be known, adopted an attitude almost identical to European colonists. In one of the great ironies of the age, they often proved to be more exclusive and segregationist than almost any European colonial power of the age.

At the same time, when Joseph Jenkins Roberts assumed office as the first President of the Liberian Republic, he found himself embroiled in a series of boundary disputes with those very European powers which somewhat projected the new black republic into the modern age. In 1840, the only French possessions in Africa were the communes of Saint-Louis, Dakar, and Goree in what would today be modern Senegal. Having lost almost all of its overseas empires as a consequence of the Napoleonic Wars, France was now increasingly interested in Africa, and the established trading networks of West Africa were of particular interest. Much in the same way Liberia was established, French land acquisitions and annexations were achieved by the purchase of land from local chiefs in often spurious transactions, supported by no less spurious treaties. In this way, French mercantile exporters began acquiring small pockets of land along the Pepper Coast, establishing satellite settlements over which the French flag flew. To counter these minor incursions, Liberia had no army to speak of no Fixed boundary delineations and certainly no international support.

To counter these minor incursions, Liberia had no army to speak of, no fixed boundary delineations, and certainly no international support.

British interests in supporting and protecting Sierra Leone as a slave colony did not extend to Liberia. This was in part because Liberia was black-ruled, unlike Sierra Leone, which was ruled as a British colony by an appointed governor. As a black republic, therefore, Liberia was up for grabs like any other black region of Africa, which meant appealing to international law for protection seemed at the time to be rather ludicrous.

French acquisitions remained minor and piecemeal, so Roberts, then Governor of the Liberian Commonwealth, spearheaded a campaign to gain legal title, through a treaty, to as much of the interior as he could.

The process was successful and is perhaps Roberts' greatest legacy. Although interior boundaries remained vague, the coastal boundary was then only slightly smaller than it is today. The money expended in all of these purchases was provided by the various colonization societies, and as such, it was something of a golden age for Liberia.

Dealing with the French was one thing, but the British posed a much more formidable obstacle. When Roberts attempted to impose customs duties on British merchant vessels in Liberian treaty zones, a Royal Navy Atlantic Squadron warship was dispatched to Monrovia from Freetown with a communication for Roberts, essentially telling him to mind his manners and not to interfere with British trade interests. Roberts responded by ordering the seizure of a Liberian ship in Liberian waters, which was promptly followed by the British seizure of a Liberian ship.

For a while, it seemed that matters could escalate, but in due course, the U.S. government issued a formal protest. As the only nation that recognized Liberia, this was something of a seminal moment. Britain confirmed that it did not recognize Liberian sovereignty, which for the time being at least, it regarded as nothing more than the commercial experiment of a philanthropic organization. A minor diplomatic spat ensued between London and Washington, but perhaps because the British wielded such significant influence in the region and the U.S. was certainly never going to forcefully intervene, the matter was left for the British and the Liberians to resolve. After all, Liberia was not a colony of the U.S., but ostensibly an independent republic.

Fortunately for the Liberians, the British were concerned mainly with other overseas interests, particularly India, British North America, and further south in Africa. Furthermore, the Crimean War would divert British attention in 1853, along with most of the empire's military and naval assets.

At whatever point Liberia constituted itself as a state with definite boundaries and responsibilities, the British hinted at the possibility of recognition, but for now, such recognition was withheld.

Meanwhile, Roberts was preoccupied with more than just the Europeans. As he was busy establishing the territorial boundaries of Liberia, he was also formulating the political structure of the Republic. At the time, the Republic of Maryland stood separate from Liberia, although three members representing Maryland sat in the Liberian lower house and the territory was represented by two senators in the Liberian senate. The Liberian political establishment was dominated by two parties: the Liberian Party and the "True Whig Party," both dominated by Americo-Liberian communities, many of mixed race. The Liberian Party could perhaps be described as a "democratic" party, while the True Whig Party was much more elitist. The True Whig Party drew most of its support from wealthier merchants and professionals, as well as the government and civil service.

In 1850, Britain extended recognition to the Republic, acknowledging Liberia's right to levy duties and taxes. On behalf of the British, a treaty of recognition was signed by the Under Secretary of State for the Colonies, one of the British Liberals, and it was perhaps fortunate that both he and the British Prime Minister, Lord Palmerston, were well to the left of the British establishment.

By the 1850s, it can reasonably be said that Liberia enjoyed international recognition. The only nation that dragged its heels, purely because it was unwilling to host a Black Liberian diplomat, was the U.S. As a result, American recognition of Liberia didn't come until 1862.

CHAPTER II

My Childhood/Family

My parents, James D. Cassell, Sr., and Marie Augusta Coleman-Cassell, were the best parents any child could ask for. Going back to my childhood, growing up in Liberia in the fifties and the sixties, seemed normal, but also very interesting. As far as I can recall, I grew up in a two-parent household with both my father and mother present and seven siblings. My father obviously was the head of our household and also the sole provider. My father used to always tell me if all of their children had survived, they would have had twelve children. Unfortunately, our mother suffered four miscarriages out of twelve pregnancies; only eight of us survived. I was the third child and the first of four girls. I had two older brothers, two younger brothers, and three younger sisters.

My father and mother both came from large families. My father's parents were Dr. Nathaniel Henry Benedict

My parents...

James David Cassell, Sr. and Marie Augusta Coleman-Cassell.

Cassell, Ph.D., and Clara Richards-Cassell. My father was the fourth of eight surviving children. I learned that our paternal grandmother also suffered multiple miscarriages. My mother, on the other hand, was a child who grew up in a large family household on her father's side. She used to tell me that her mother, who was a single mom, gave birth to two children, a girl and a boy from different fathers. Her father and stepmother raised her from the age of seven when her mother took her to Monrovia to live with her father. She also told me she grew up in a large house with many siblings—brothers and sisters—on her father's side. The William David Coleman family home was in the city of Monrovia on a street named Coleman Hill. It was a big house with many occupants. My grandfather was wealthy or well-off, very kind, and charismatic. Her father and my grandfather had twenty-two children and approximately twenty-eight to thirty grandchildren.

My grandfather on my father's side, Dr. Nathaniel H.B. Cassell, Ph.D., was a pastor and an educator. He was a co-founder and president of The Liberian College (1918-1934), currently known as The University of Liberia. Unfortunately, I never got to know my grandfather because he passed away before I was born. I remember in the 1960s a library was built on the campus of The University of Liberia and was named The Cassell building in his honor as one of the founding members of the University. As one of his oldest granddaughters, I was selected to cut the ribbon at the official opening ceremony. As a teenager, it was a great honor for me to be in the presence of dignitaries, educators, government officials, and family members. At the ceremony, I had to give a speech written by my father which I had to memorize. This was a great moment for a teenage girl back in the sixties. I made my parents and other family members very proud. My grandfather was a highly educated and intelligent man.

I also didn't know my grandmother, Clara Richards-Cassell, because she passed away when I was an infant. I remembered my father telling me she was a wife, homemaker, and a very good mother who raised nine children.

Our family roots in Liberia on both my father's and mother's sides go back to the migration of the freed slaves who returned to their roots in West Africa. My father's grandparents, the Cassells, arrived in Liberia in one of two slave ships which settled on a piece of land off the Atlantic Ocean. The second ship carrying the other Cassell brother settled in Freetown, Sierra Leone, one of the neighboring countries. Ancestors from both sides of our family were referred to as Americo-Liberians, who were considered or referred to as the privileged class.

My great grandfather on my mother's side, William David Coleman, was the twelfth President of the Republic of Liberia from 1896 to 1900.

CHAPTER III

My Early Education

My primary and secondary education was in Liberia. Established under the western system, and our primary language was and is English in the school system. Because of the country's history, the education systems were and continue to be modeled after the U.S. education system. The freed slaves who settled in Liberia in the 19th century brought with them the knowledge they had learned from the United States education system, adapted and made their system a staple in the country. We learned from the same textbooks. The Liberian government, which controls the system, received a lot of help from the U.S. government. They later got help for teachers from the American Peace Corps. We also used the same grading systems in schools and classrooms.

My siblings and I attended primary and secondary private schools. I graduated from St. Teresa's Convent, a girls-only Catholic high school. It was a boarding and a day school run by nuns. I attended daily classes. I was an above-average student who loved to learn and enjoyed going to school every day. I had my share of friends and loved participating in school activities, sports, such as track and field, softball, volleyball, and almost all social events. I loved music and dancing, enjoying different genres, especially R&B, Motown, Soul, Highlife/West African and Caribbean music.

Unfortunately, in my last year of high school, I lost my father suddenly to a massive heart attack. This was devastating for our mother and the entire family. He left behind a widow and eight children. As a little girl growing up, I used to tell my father, who was a lawyer, that I wanted to be a lawyer like him, and he used to encourage me to be an international lawyer. Since I was the only one of his eight children who wanted to follow in his steps, he was very proud of me and used to tell me he was going to put me through college and law school even if he had to sell the last shirt off his back.

I had a very close bond with my father and losing him at a young age felt like a knife had been stuck in my heart, and my life's plan to become a lawyer died with him. After his death, my dreams were crushed. I felt like I wouldn't make it to college because I had no financial support. I couldn't depend on my mother, who was a widow and had never worked a full-time day job outside the home in her entire life and now had to take care of five of her eight children still at home, who depended on her for support. Losing my father left a huge void in my life.

Growing up in the fifties and sixties, I have to credit a lot of who I am today to my parents, especially my father who always talked to me about everything he learned and read about what was going on in the world we lived in and what was going on in the U.S., which was considered our mother country. That our country was founded, built, and modeled after the U.S.A. First and foremost, English became the official language. Our government and school system were based on the U.S./western system. Even our flag colors—red, white, and blue—are very similar to the U.S. flag by design.

My father was an avid reader and encouraged me to read early in my life. He used to bring home and read every U.S. magazine, such as *Time*, *Newsweek*, *Life*, *Ebony* and *Jet*, and every book he could get his hands on. Almost every weekday we would sit at our dining room table after dinner, finishing our homework, and he would talk with me for a few hours. I used to feel like he knew more about what was happening in the U.S. than a lot of Americans who lived there. He used to tell me that in the future, people will be able to see each other while talking on the telephone, and robots, not people, will be cleaning the house. Exactly what is happening today many years later. I used to say to myself, "What is he talking about?" During that time, it seemed like *Mission Impossible*. Today, living in this world, realizing and seeing how fast time is passing and how things are changing, like technology, the internet, the unbelievable advancements in medicine and social media, I can truly say that my father was way ahead of his time.

He would talk with me about current events and just about everything that was happening around the world and in the U.S., especially in the fifties and sixties, during the civil rights movement, the fight for voting and equal rights, Martin Luther King Jr., his constant fight and struggles for freedom for the Negroes. Equality for all people of color in the U.S. and around the world. He told me about the history of slavery and what the Negroes people were experiencing in this country, like he lived in the U.S. instead of Liberia, West Africa. Being an avid reader, he told me a lot about slavery and how white people treated Negroes in America, how men, women, and children were lynched and beaten to death because of the color of their skin.

He also told me that in the U.S., if a person had as little as 1% Negro blood, they were considered Negro. Some of those Negroes who were very light-skinned and could pass as white would disown their family because they would rather hide their identity and live a better life. On April 4, 1968, I remembered my father telling me that Dr. Martin Luther King, Jr. had been assassinated in Memphis, Tennessee. This was another very sad news to hear five years after the assassination of President John F. Kennedy. Dr. King was a pastor and civil rights leader who lost his life fighting for something he strongly believed in, hoping to change the lives of Black people and all people of color in this world. He devoted his life's work to the civil rights movement, starting in the South, in states such as Alabama, Georgia, and Mississippi, to name a few. He was a fearless and great leader who strongly believed in the practice of non-violence. He was pastor of Ebenezer Baptist Church in Atlanta, Georgia, a church he inherited from his father, who was also a pastor. I learned a lot about Dr. King's life and work from my father. Growing up in Liberia, I read and listened to many of his speeches, especially one of his most famous "I Have a Dream" which is well known all over the world. Sometimes, my father used to compare him to Jesus Christ on earth. Another one of his quotes, I will always remember, is "The quality, not the longevity of one's life is what is important."

CHAPTER IV

Coming to America (Summer 1969)

About a year after I graduated from high school and the death of my father, I found myself on a plane to the United States of America. Without my father but with a lot of prayers, hard work, determination, and support from my family, especially my mother, I worked and also raised money to get a ticket and just enough money for tuition to cover at least my first semester at Langston University, an HBCU, in Langston, Oklahoma.

I arrived at John F. Kennedy International Airport on August 21, 1969, in New York City. I spent about two weeks in Queens, New York, with family before heading to Langston. My cousin, Kathleen, and I, accompanied by our aunt Eleanor, flew to Langston in time to start the fall semester of 1969. Even though they were male students from Africa, we were the first African women to attend Langston University, making history and hoping we wouldn't be the last.

Before I left Liberia, the current Liberian Secretary of Education had promised my mom that I would be awarded a full scholarship from the Liberian government to continue my education in the United States at Langston, which didn't happen. My mother and I were very disappointed because they kept giving us the runaround and false hope. After the first semester ended in December at Langston University and I had no scholarship funds to continue and complete the first year of college, I told my mom to stop letting them give her the runaround and stop listening to their lies.

I knew I had to leave Langston and make other plans to continue my education. So, I asked my aunt Eleanor, who lived upstate in Poughkeepsie, New York, with her family if I could come live with her for a little while until I could raise money to get back to school. She graciously agreed and practically saved me from becoming homeless, and I am forever grateful and thankful to her.

Since I had no money, Aunt Eleanor helped me get a job at the telephone company in Poughkeepsie as a long-distance operator. I lived with her and her family while working and saving every dime I could for nine months, from January 1970 to September 1970. I saved sufficient money to move to Los Angeles, California, which was my dream place to live in the U.S. to start a new life for myself and to continue my college education.

I never gave up on my dreams of finishing college.

CHAPTER V

My Life in Los Angeles, California

I arrived in Los Angeles, California, at Los Angeles International Airport (LAX) in September 1970. The moment I landed in Los Angeles, I fell in love with the city. Palm trees lined the streets. The weather was always wonderful, with no snow or cold to freezing temperatures. The palm trees reminded me of the tropical climate back home where I grew up in Liberia, West Africa. It surely is my dream place to live.

Especially when I actually went to the corner of Hollywood and Vine, the intersection of Hollywood Boulevard and Vine Street in Hollywood, a place I had read about and dreamed of visiting as a little girl growing up thousands of miles away in West Africa. I had to pinch myself to make sure I wasn't waking up from a dream and this was real.

My first home was at the Evangeline Residence for Women in downtown Los Angeles, a room and board facility for young women moving to the big city and needing a secure and affordable place to live. A good friend who had been living in Los Angeles for several years recommended it to me.

About two to three months after I moved to Los Angeles, I experienced my first earthquake one night while lying in my bed trying to go to sleep. I felt the bed shaking and was a little afraid and wondering what was going on because this was something I had never experienced, not knowing that I was experiencing an active earthquake. The shaking lasted for only a few minutes, which felt like forever. I got up after it stopped and looked under my bed to see what in the world was causing my bed to shake and if someone was under my bed. I didn't see anybody or anything under my bed that would cause the shaking I had felt. Somehow I fell asleep.

I had to get up early to go to work and school. I didn't find out that the shaking I felt was an earthquake until the next morning after I went downstairs to the dining room for breakfast. While sitting at a table with some ladies, I heard them talking about the earthquake they felt last night. I realized I had experienced my first earthquake in Los Angeles, California, which I will never forget.

CHAPTER VI

My College Education

I was accepted at The University of Southern California (U.S.C.) in the Undergraduate School of Business program about a year before I moved to Los Angeles. Unfortunately, I could not attend the University because I didn't receive the academic scholarship promised by the Liberian government's Secretary of Education. To get back into college and continue my education, after a year of living and working in Poughkeepsie, New York, I attended Sawyer College of Business, a two-year business college in downtown Los Angeles, where I was also living at the Evangeline residence, which was very close to the school.

I graduated with honors after two years and earned an Associate of Arts Degree in Airline Operations and a minor in accounting. Despite facing struggles, living on my own in a big city like Los Angeles, I worked odd jobs to support myself, pay the rent, and keep food on the table. Determined to make it on my own, I refused to depend on anyone else. Remembering my parents' advice to get an education and not be afraid of hard work, I persevered.

After graduating from Sawyer College, I continued my education at Pacific States University from February 18, 1974 to June 14, 1975, and graduated magna cum laude with a Bachelor of Arts Degree in Business Administration. While attending Pacific States, I worked full-time at Wells Fargo Bank and attended classes in the evenings and at night.

Without any financial resources or support, I had to do it on my own. Utilizing the bank's tuition refund program, I applied for and received a refund every semester after passing my classes with a 3.0 GPA or better. This program allowed me to graduate froMCollege with zero student loan debt.

CHAPTER VII

My Career in Banking

After going to many interviews looking for a job in banking and being told that I had no experience, I got my first full job at Citizen Bank, a community bank in Mid-City Los Angeles. It was an entry-level position as the branch's Bookkeeper. After a year on that job, I was promoted to the consumer loan credit department as a credit checker and assistant to the branch's Assistant Manager. My job was to process new consumer loan applications, order credit reports, and submit all applications to the Assistant Manager for approval. Shortly after I got promoted to the position and moved to the branch's platform from the operation department, the bank got robbed by four guys who surprised everybody including the customers in the bank by walking in the bank front doors with guns demanding everybody including the customers to put both hands up and don't move and be still. One of the robbers jumped over the counter on the teller's operation side of the bank and demanded the tellers to open their draws, and he took all the cash he could get. One of theMCame over to the platform which was on the opposite side of the branch where I was working and pointed his gun directly at my face. I was afraid, envious, and shacking, he told me to be cool and don't move. I thought I was going to die especially since I had never ever experienced or seen a gun that close up pointed directly at me. At that time, I started to pray and asked God to save me. He answered my prayer.

After what seemed like an eternity, one of the robbers who were guiding the front door yelled out that they had to get out of the bank at that moment before the Cops arrived. Apparently, somebody in the bank had pulled the silent alarm they were on their way. They got all the cash they could from the teller draws and ran out of the bank, just before the police arrived. The experience was like a nightmare I will never forget. Thank God nobody got shot or hurt in this bank robbery. The robbers were eventually arrested, tried, and sent to prison. Oh, by the way, the robbers were young black guys and they got only four thousand dollars, which wasn't worth robbing a bank and going to jail for a long time.

After working at that bank for about two years, one day a customer, who was an African-American older woman, came up to my desk at the bank and gave me the business card of a bank manager at the Wells Fargo Bank branch in Santa Monica, California. She told me that I should be working at that branch in Santa Monica instead of where I was currently working. She told me to call the manager Mr. John Moore, an African-American. I thanked her and did exactly what she told me to do. I called him got an interview and was hired for my first teller position at the bank. After working at the Wells Fargo branch in Santa Monica for a year and a half, I decided to transfer to another branch on Wilshire Blvd closer to where I lived in south-central Los Angeles. The new branch was in the Miracle Mile prestige business district on Wilshire Boulevard.

While working at that branch, I decided to go back to school at night to get a B.A. Degree in Business Administration. I applied and was accepted at Pacific States University in Los Angeles. I worked full-time and attended classes after working four nights a week. It wasn't easy, but I was determined to get my degree.

I completed my degree and graduated Magna Cum Laude on June 6, 1975. A few months after I received my degree, I decided it was time to advance my career in banking. I applied for a position as a trainee in the bank's annual management training program to become a bank officer ultimately, a branch manager. I was told that as a current bank employee, I had to get a letter of recommendation from my immediate supervisor and the branch manager, who were both white. Even though I was highly qualified for the position with over five years of experience in banking and a B.A. Degree in Business

Administration, I was very surprised after I requested a letter of recommendation from my supervisor and was denied for no legitimate reason except that I was a victim of discrimination. At first, I was surprised and disappointed because I was not expecting that response, and getting this job meant a lot to me and my career. It took me a few days to process the situation.

After dealing with their rejection over and over in my mind, I decided that I was going to fight for the job. I spoke to a good friend and mentor who was one of the few African-American male branch managers, I had met working at Wells Fargo Bank and told him what had happened after I had asked my supervisor and manager for a letter of recommendation, and their surprised response. He was also surprised and asked me what reasons they gave me for refusing to recommend me because I was highly qualified for the position. I told him they gave me none which made no sense.

He told me to ask them to put it in writing. I did exactly what he said and asked for a meeting with the branch manager the next day and looked him directly in his face and told him exactly how I felt, that they were discriminating against me, and that I was not going to let them get away with it.

In the meantime, I was trying to figure out how I was going to get an interview for the position I really wanted. A bank customer, who happened to be a Civil Rights Attorney and an African American, worked at a law office located in the same building as the bank's branch. He had previously told a co-worker of mine who happened to be an African American female and a bank teller, that if we ever felt that we were victims of any discrimination on the job to give him a call. He left his business card with her.

After I told her about the situation, she gave me his card and encouraged me to call him. We were the only two African American tellers working at that branch. I immediately called and told him about the refusal of my supervisor and the branch manager to write a letter recommending me as an employee for a trainee position in the bank's management training program.

I knew that I was qualified for the position and strongly felt that their refusal was a sign of discrimination and needed some advice on what I could do to get the job without their recommendation.

About a week after our conversation, he wrote an unsolicited letter of recommendation on my behave to the Assistant Vice President at the Bank's Southern California corporate office in El Monte who was in charge of hiring qualified candidates for the training program. A few days after the letter was delivered, I got a phone call at the branch from the A.V.P. himself who made an appointment with me to meet him for an interview.

I was very excited and made an announcement to everybody in the branch: "I got the interview." The interview went very well. One question he asked during the interview, which I will never forget, was "Tell me what you have done to prepare yourself for this job." After I answered his question, telling him about my work experience in banking, a B.A. Degree in Business Admin./finance, etc., he said that he had asked many candidates the same question and no one else had answered as I did. A few days after the interview, he called and offered me a position as a trainee in the bank's management training program. During the interview, he also said that he usually interviews between 300-400 candidates annually for about 20-30 positions for the bank's management training program and I was one of the most qualified candidates he had interviewed for the position.

A couple of months after I got the call and was offered a position in the program, I was excited to start my new job. The bank officers' training program was yearlong. Each trainee was assigned to a branch at different locations every month. We had to learn every job in the branch by sitting with the employee at his or her desk, who showed the trainee how to do their job hands-on, moving on the next month to the next branch to learn the next job and so on. The goal was that every trainee had to learn every job in the branch.

In addition to the branch training, once every month all the trainees had to travel, to the bank's corporate office in San Francisco, all expenses paid, to meet in a formal setting with an instructor and trainees from the north and south we also did roll plays.

Upon completion of the year's training, we were assigned to a branch to work as a Consumer Loan Officer. Our jobs or duties were to assist customers who applied for consumer or auto loans, secured or unsecured. The customer would submit a loan application, which would usually be reviewed, processed, and approved or denied by the Loan Officer.

After four years of working in branch banking at Wells Fargo Bank, I was beginning to realize that chances for advancement, especially for African American women, including me, were very limited. So, I decided it was time to move on in order to advance my career in banking. I made a decision to update my resume and applied for a position at Bank of America, the largest bank at that time, in the U.S.

In February 1978, I got interviewed and was offered a position in Bank of America's Advanced Management training program. I completed the program in six months and was assigned to work at a branch in Whittier, California as a Bank Loan Officer. My duties were to evaluate and approve consumer and business loan applications, follow up and maintain lines of credit for preferred corporate and small business customers such as medium to large auto dealerships in the branch service area, analyze financial statements for major accounts, and responsible for up to $25+ million portfolios, made weekly business development visits to new and existing customers.

While still working at Bank of America in Whittier, California, on July 4,1980, I married the love of my life,

Gary Franklin Austin. It was a beautiful wedding with many family members attending, my mother and grandmother, who traveled from West Africa, four of my dearest Aunties flew in from the east coast, New York, and Maryland, my big brother, James and his wife Gwendolyn and many others. The ceremony as well as the reception was held at the Ministry Chapel in Hollywood, California, with an outdoor open area in the back of the Chapel, where the wedding reception was held.

I was overjoyed to have my family and friends there to celebrate this very special occasion in my life. It was one of the happiest days of my life.

On December 28, 1980, I gave birth to a healthy 9-pound, 5-ounce baby girl our firstborn. We named her Gwendolyn Patricia Austin II, after me because Gary and I decided since she was our firstborn, if we had a boy he would be named after him and if a girl, she would be named after me. We nicknamed her "Tricia" mainly because we thought it would be a little less confusing in our house with the two of us answering to the same name at the same time. Gary was a great father and husband who was very proud and loving and worked hard to take care of his family. Whenever he had some free time, he would take our beautiful baby girl out and show her off to everybody they came in contact with because he was so proud to be a father. Unfortunately, he didn't live long to see her grow up. We lost him on January 6, 1986, a month after her fifth birthday.

His passing was very shocking and difficult for us and his family. He was in his thirties and was gone too soon. He was full of life, very funny, always making me and everyone around him laugh. I used to always tell him that he missed hiMCalling. He should have been a comedian. It was very difficult to explain losing him to our five-year-old daughter.

I experienced discrimination on the job again, working at Bank of America, this time from my immediate supervisor. Who was a white male and former Truck Driver turned banker. I knew that I was doing an excellent job because of my work ethic, and interaction with my co-workers and customers who always appreciated my professional service and always thanked me.

I noticed that after several job performance reviews from him as my immediate supervisor, I never got a level one or two performance evaluation from him. Instead, he always gave me a level three which was considered average on a scale of one to five and was also used to determine how much my salary increase would be. After my last performance evaluation, I asked him why I never got a level one or two performance evaluation from him, I was very surprised by his answer, he told me in order to get a higher performance review such as a one or two, I had to finish my work and do some of the other employee work. I told him the bank wasn't paying me enough for the job I was already doing. After that conversation, I realized that I was never going to get paid what I was worth as long as I was working under a racist like him.

At that time, I was seven months pregnant with our first child and was about to take a six-month maternity leave. I told myself at the end of my leave, that I was not going back to that job, or at that branch, to continue working under that racist jerk.

At the end of my six-month maternity leave, I turned in my letter of resignation. With my husband Gary working full time supporting our family, I decided to return to graduate school to earn my Master in Business Administration (M.B.A.) at West Coast University in Los Angeles, Wilshire District near downtown. I enrolled in their evening classes designed for business professionals who wanted to keep their jobs while fulfilling their dreams of achieving a higher degree to advance their career. This decision allowed me the time and opportunity to take care of my baby at home during the day and attend classes at night while my husband Gary watched our daughter at night.

On March 6, 1982, I successfully completed my required classes and graduated with an in Business (M.B.A.) Degree. After graduating, I decided it was time to return to work. I quickly realized it wasn't easy to find a good-paying professional job after being in the workforce for a little over two years. I was facing many challenges that I wasn't expecting, especially with my background, education, and experience in banking. I mailed out many resumes and went on many interviews but, I wasn't getting any of the job offers I was expecting. I remember being told that the main reason was that I had been out of the workforce too long.

Even though during the off time I was attending college and working on my Master's Degree in Business & Finance, it didn't matter to employers who made it difficult to get the job I really wanted and had worked so hard to get. At that point, I was beginning to feel a little frustrated.

I was determined to get back to work and refused to let disappointment get the best of me. So, I kept going to job interviews until I finally got a job at First Pacific Bank in Los Angeles. The position was a Real Estate Loan Manager Assistant. I was responsible for packaging and processing all types of real estate loans including residential, commercial, and construction. I worked there from December 1982 through January 31, 1984. This wasn't my dream job.

However, I was able to get back into the workforce to get some experience in real estate financing, which later became an asset in my career. In some way, this job was a blessing. It was also the starting point of what turned out to be my career in real estate financing where I found my purpose and enjoyed helping people purchase their first or second home or investment property.

I fell in love with it and the rest is history. Sadly, after two years on this job, I was laid off because the bank was going through some financial problems and had to close their real estate department.

CHAPTER VIII

My Career in Real Estate Financing and R.E. Investment

At the beginning of my real estate financing career, I worked at several financial institutions banks, savings and loans associations and mortgage banks. I learned a lot from the job training. During that time, I began to realize the potential and my ability to build generational wealth through real estate investments. As soon as the opportunities prevailed, I was able to save enough to purchase my first piece of property. I started looking for single-family houses, 2-4 family residential units that I could buy. I was able to purchase my first piece of property, a small duplex in 1975 for a price of only $29,500, with 2-1 bedrooms, and 1 bath. I applied and qualified for a 90% conventional bank loan with 10% down payment plus closing cost from my savings. The property needed cleaning, painting and minor repairs or TLC before I could put it up for rent. I spent approximately fifteen hundred dollars to fix up the property. I was able to rent both units for sufficient income to pay the mortgage, property taxes, insurance, and maintenance expenses.

Two years later, after the property value appreciated, I sold the property for $60,000, double my original cost and netted approximately $22,000 from the sale after all expenses were paid. This marked the beginning of my real estate investment career.

In 1981, my husband Gary and I decided to purchase a two-story duplex, each with 2 bedrooms and 1 bathroom, with a large backyard. We moved into one of the units as our primary residence, with our baby girl and a dog.

We stopped paying rent and became homeowners as well as landlords. This was very exciting for us, and it felt good to become new homeowners instead of renters.

After I was laid off from my job at First Pacific Bank in January 1984. In February 1984, I got a new job at Corpuz and Associates, an independent loan agent for California Federal Savings and Loan Assn.

One of the largest savings and loans in California. My job was as a loan agent assistant. I worked there from February 1984 to July 30, 1984. I Quit after five months of working there for a couple of reasons, I was unhappy with the salary and felt that it was too low, and I was under pay for the work I was during. I decided to apply for and got a much better job.

CHAPTER IX

Becoming a Mortgage Loan Sales Representative

In July 1984, I got a job interview at RNG Mortgage Company in La Palma, California, a thirty-minute drive from where I lived in Los Angeles.

This interview turned out to be the interview that changed my life. The job I applied for was for an underwriter's position paying a starting salary of $2000 per month plus benefits. The manager who interviewed me was very impressed with me and proceeded to tell me about a loan officer position instead. Based on my background and experience, she felt that I was a perfect fit for the loan officer position. She also told me that I could earn up to $6000 per month. Three times higher than the Underwriter job I had initially applied for. She told me in order to qualify for the loan officer position, I had to get a California Real Estate Sales license which I didn't have and had to get if I wanted the job. She said in order to get a real estate sales license quickly, I could take a crash course in real estate sales and get my license in 4-6 weeks. I had to sign up for the course which was held on the weekend, all day Saturday and Sunday, and follow up by taking sample tests at a Coldwell Banker Real Estate Office in Los Angeles. Depending on how fast I could pace myself to complete the course, I could be ready to take the State Exam in 3-4 weeks and start earning commissions right away. I decided that it was worth it, and I did it and accepted the position on the condition that I would get my real estate sales license as quickly as possible.

The fact that I could earn up to $6000 per month with this job after I got my state real estate sales license was motivating and exciting to me. I was very excited, and nothing could stop me especially since I was currently earning less than $2000 per month at my previous jobs. I felt that I was on my way to a successful career in real estate financing. I studied and worked very hard and within six weeks I took the state of California Real Estate sales exam, passed with flying colors, and got my license. This job was surely the beginning of a successful real estate financing career for me, and I never looked back.

I felt that I was well on my way to building generational wealth in real estate and finance for myself and my family. Since this was my first ever job in sales, I decided to take some training classes in sales. I had to get up from behind a desk and the comfort of my office and go out into the fields daily to call on prospective clients. Introduce myself and meet and talk with strangers, such as real estate brokers and agents, in an effort to build relationships and trust. It wasn't easy trying to convince strangers to trust you with their clients and their livelihoods.

For the first time, I was about to take a commission-only job. No wages or salary. I would get paid after the loan closed. NO CLOSE, NO PAY, NO EAT! Starting as a new Loan Officer in this job normally takes about 2-4 months to earn your first commission check. However, that didn't discourage me. I worked hard every day, long hours with my eyes on the prize and one goal in mind to become successful with no limits. On November 16, 1984, my original real estate sales license was issued. The next day, I started working as a commission-only Mortgage Sales Loan Officer.

As a Mortgage Loan Officer, I was responsible for soliciting and originating all types of real estate loans, including conventional and government loans (FHA & VA). Providing financing on purchase of S.F.R., 2-4 units and multifamily residential properties (5-plus units). I worked closely with loan processors and underwriters to get loans from origination to approval, funding, and closing.

In my first year, I originated an average of 15-20 loans per month closed an average of 12-15 loans and achieved a top producer award. I also achieved my commission goal of

6,000 to $7000 per month. This job was like a dreaMCome true for me. RNG Mortgage Company was the first mortgage company I worked for as a sales commission Loan Officer from November 1984 to February 1987. Earning the highest commission in my career during that time. Learning and gaining valuable experience and achieving success in a field, I felt very comfortable and motivated doing. Especially helping ordinary working people and their families in my community achieve their American dreams of homeownership, which could alternately gain and accomplish generational worth.

After three years at RNG Mortgage as a successful Mortgage Loan Officer, I decided to move on to banks in my community and closer to home.

CHAPTER X

First Job as a Mortgage Loan Agent

For a Loan Agent position at Great Western Bank, the second largest savings and loan mortgage bank in California at that time. I interviewed and got the job Mortgage Loan Agent, which also turned out to be another one of my dream jobs. Within my first year, I worked very hard all my way to the top and became the top Loan Agent at the LA Crenshaw branch. At this location I was much closer to home, spending less time in traffic commuting, which made me very happy. This job allows me to build a successful network among Real Estate Brokers and Agents in my community. Originating on average 30-35 new loan applications per month and closing 25-30 loans per month. Consistently maintaining the top 20 producer status in the Southern California region, funding and closing on average $3.8-$4.0 million dollars monthly. I really enjoyed working at Great Western Bank, especially at the LA/Baldwin Hills

Crenshaw branch located in the heart of the African American community, giving me the opportunity to work with people in my community. Assisting first-time homebuyers achieve the American dreams of homeownership, building equity and wealth in real estate for their families.

In the eighties, nineties and early two thousand (20th century), I focused on working hard building a brand as well as a reputation, becoming one of the top mortgage loan agents in the African American community. Which turned out to be a great referral base and thriving professional relationships among the best of the best in the African American real estate market. In the late eighties to the nineties, while becoming well known as a successful mortgage Loan Agent I was being sought after by headhunters and was also being approached with offers from other savings and loans, mortgage bankers opening new branches in our community. My first response was no because I was during very well with my current employer and not interested in leaving my current job. However, they were determined and wouldn't take no for an answer. After several months of ignoring and resisting them, I agreed to an interview with a Regional Manager at American Savings Bank. She told me they were about to open a new branch in the newly opened Baldwin Hills Crenshaw Mall and were looking to hire a Sales Manager for the loan center. They had done their search for a well-qualified and experienced person well known in the community. As a top producer, I was highly recommended for the job. I told her that I was grateful for being considered, but I wasn't interested in leaving my current employer. They didn't give up. Several weeks later we had a second meeting, and they made me an offer I couldn't refuse. After some negotiation back and forth, we agreed on a package which included exactly what I wanted to make the move.

CHAPTER XI

Advanced Career in Real Estate Mortgage Loan Sales

Iaccepted their offer and position as Assistant Vice President and Sales Manager, which included a salary plus commission with a benefit package.

I resigned from my job at Great Western Bank as of December 31, 1990, and started my new job at American Savings Bank on January 3, 1991. For the first time, my job included two positions and two titles, Assistant Vice President and Loan Center Sales Manager, a salary position. My second position was Mortgage Loan Consultant, commission only on all loans I personally originated and closed. This was part of the agreement I negotiated with the bank's top executives who were part of the team that got me to make the move from Great Western to American Savings Bank. A working manager which was a new position created for the first time in the bank's history. In my position as Assistant Vice President

Sales Manager, I was responsible for managing the newly opened loan center in Los Angeles Baldwin Hills Crenshaw Mall. I managed four to five Loan Consultants and several office personnel. I was also originating and closing loans. I was personally originating and bringing in new business. I was able to maintain business relationships I had established with Real Estate Brokers and Agents over the years working in the community. I worked with bank customers as needed to ensure proper and professional customer service. Oversee all loans originated and closed in our loan center.

I achieved President's Club Award in 1992 and Top Producer Award in the Metro Valley Region from 1992 to 1994 for the most closed and most purchase ARM transactions closed. While working at American Savings Bank in the early to late nineties, Washington Mutual Bank bought American Savings and Great Western Bank. I continued working at Washington Mutual as a Loan Consultant until May 15, 1997, when I resigned to open my Mortgage Brokerage Company.

On March 3, 1997, I received my Real Estate Broker license from the California Department of Real Estate, which qualified me to open my mortgage brokerage company.

CHAPTER XII

Becoming an Entrepreneur—The Beginning of a New Chapter

On September 1, 1997, I opened my new company: Viewpointe Funding Group, Inc., a mortgage brokerage firm, located at 3700 Wilshire Boulevard, suite 574, Los Angeles, California, in the heart of the Wilshire business district, 10-15 minutes from the downtown Los Angeles, with a business partner, whose name I will not mention.

After about 8-10 months into the partnership, I quickly realized that it was not a good fit and was not working out like I expected, for several reasons. So, before the situation got worse and out of hand, I decided it was time to resolve the partnership and go our separate ways.

I immediately formed a new company under the name of Pointe of View International Inc. and moved to a new suite #625 in the same building where I was officially on my own. After I settled in my own space, I was happy and on my

way to operating a successful mortgage business. I hired and trained my sister, Mai, as a loan processor and eventually the Office manager and my oldest daughter, Gwendolyn II (nicknamed Tricia), as a junior loan processor and office assistant. I also recruited and hired several licensed Real Estate Sales Agents who were independent contractors and were paid a commission on all sales deals they originated and closed. The first year of opening my new office turned out to be very successful, which I credited to the strong relationships and trust I was able to build and maintain over many years among Real Estate Brokers and Agents in my community.

Many of them were willing to support the new company and keep the business coming. At that point in my career as a business owner during very well, I felt like my dreams had come true and were on top of the world. But also realized that getting there took a lot of hard work, long hours even working on the weekends.

I loved my new office space and location. Some days sitting in my office on the sixth floor looking out the large glass windows on Wilshire Boulevard, one of the most known and popular business districts in Los Angeles. Had always been a dream place for me to open my business and to work. One Wilshire Boulevard started from downtown Los Angeles to Santa Monica Beach, a 15. 9 miles east to west and one of the longest boulevards in the city. It was a beautiful sight to see at least five days a week. I loved what I did for a living and my career. As a committed Mortgage Loan Broker. Always motivated me to wake up every morning and go out there with the desire to help as many people as I could to achieve the American dream of homeownership. I strongly felt that I was making a small contribution to society seeing the pure joy and happiness on the faces of a client after going through and completing the long, daunting process of purchasing their first home. It was very satisfying and rewarding for me.

I mentioned earlier that the first year of opening my business was a huge success ending the year with gross earnings in six figures, which gave me the opportunity to expand my Real Estate Investments. Increasing my investment properties portfolio.

I purchased several pieces of properties in the eighties and nineties before I opening my office. Most of the properties I purchased were income producing, single family houses, 2-4 units, multifamily residential units.

Most of the properties I bought needed to be repaired or fixed up (which is now referred to as fixed and flip) some were put up for sale after the work was done and sold for profit, netting 50 to 80 percent profit. Some of the properties was fixed up, repair and rented for sufficient Income to pay the mortgage, taxes, insurance and other expenses making a net income monthly.

Some held for investment renting to tenants for several years and sold for profits and some were held longer 10, 15, 20 years which were all income producing.

In 1989, we decided to purchase a larger home, a 3-bedroom, 2.5-bath, 1800 sq. ft., 2-story Townhouse in a gated community in Inglewood, named Briarwood Townhomes. We moved out of the 2-bedroom 1-bath duplex we purchased in 1981 and rented the unit we vacated, making it a profitable investment property. We needed a larger home to accommodate our growing family; I was pregnant with my second child, Erica, who was born on November 26, 1989.

Between 1981 to 2010, I was able to expand my real estate portfolio and accomplish my goal of becoming a licensed real estate broker in 1997, after completing and passing the State of California Broker's exam. While still working in mortgage banking at Washington Mutual Bank, I decided it was time to open my mortgage brokerage company and fulfill my dreams of becoming an entrepreneur. I was also well on my way to becoming a successful Real Estate Investor. Over time, I was able to build an impressive real estate business portfolio of approximately 20-25 properties. I took advantage of every opportunity I had to purchase real properties, including fixes and flips in the eighties and nineties when it was not as popular as it is today. Holding some for investment rentals, I was always looking for a good deal to expand my investment portfolio.

As I look back over the years, facing and overcoming many trials and tribulations, ups and downs but never giving up, I felt that I had to be strong for my two young daughters, who had lost their fathers at a very young age. I worked hard and was determined to give them the best life possible, including a good education. I was a single mother raising two daughters. Losing my first husband Gary F. Austin, the father of my first daughter, at the young age of thirty-four (34), was a tough blow. He struggled with drug addiction off and on, and I did everything I could to support him during those times.

Together we found a drug rehab center, and he signed up, determined to get the help he desperately needed to get well and become drug-free. The program was helpful for a couple of years. Shortly after, he lost his job and couldn't find another one right away, which led to depression and eventually a relapse into drug use. I was working long and hard to keep the bills paid, keep a roof over our heads, and keep our family together.

He never got over his depression, which eventually led to his death by suicide. These were very difficult times for me, a young widow in my thirties with a five-year-old child to raise. I had to focus on raising and protecting our daughter, who was too young to understand the trauma of his passing and why he had left us so early. It was very difficult trying to comfort and help her understand why he was not coming home to us. Many days, I had to hide my tears while telling her he was in heaven.

Approximately eight months after losing my dear husband Gary, I decided to go out for the first time after being invited to a summer social event hosted by one of my business associates, who was a Real Estate Broker. It felt good to get out and socialize with friends and business associates after a long time. At the event, I met a very handsome young man named Eric Freeman, who asked me to dance, introduced himself, and told me that his brother was best friends with the broker who was hosting the event. We had a good time dancing and talking all evening. We exchanged phone numbers and spent lots of time together, quickly becoming inseparable. He also told me he had just moved to California from Detroit, MI. We fell in love and got married two years later in the summer of 1988.

My life with Eric in the beginning was like a dream come true. We were crazy in love and very happy. We got married on June 25, 1988, two years after we met. Our beautiful baby girl was born on November 26, 1989. She was our Thanksgiving gift from God, our pride and joy, and a blessing. She was also a second daughter for both of us. Eric had a daughter, MeShawn, from his first marriage, and I also had a daughter, Tricia, from my first marriage to Gary. After I got pregnant with my second child, we realized that we needed more space for our growing family. We purchased a three-bedroom, two-and-a-half-bath, 1800 square feet, two-story townhouse in a gated community named Briarwood Townhomes in the city of Inglewood, CA. It was a predominantly African American community, often referred to as the black Beverly Hills. We loved our new home, especially with the additional space, moving from a 2-bedroom bath duplex. Erica was born about two weeks after we moved into our new home. Life was so wonderful; we were a happy family feeling blessed to bring our newborn baby girl, our little bundle of joy, to our new home.

Eric was a Vietnam veteran who struggled off and on like most soldiers or veterans, dealing with drug addictions and sometimes Post-Traumatic Stress (PTS). He talked about his struggle with drugs such as morphine given to soldiers to help deal with the pain and suffering they were experiencing, leading to additional problems and not getting the professional help or support they needed to cope with reality. These situations sometimes became a distraction and caused problems in many relationships and marriages.

After several years of struggling to keep our marriage and family together, raising our daughters, and working long hours to keep the bills paid and a roof over our heads, things took a turn for the worse. Eric lost his job and was having problems finding another one. He was getting to the lowest point in his life. Things deteriorated further; he started doing more drugs. Together, we decided that he had to get professional help, so he checked himself into the VA Hospital in West Los Angeles for drug rehab. He was there for about a year and a half. I was taking our six-year-old daughters to visit him almost every weekend. I wanted her to know her father and bond with him. I was getting encouraging reports about the progress he was making at the VA and was very hopeful that he would become drug-free and come home soon to his family. Little did I know that we wouldn't have that happy ending.

After spending one of our Sunday afternoons with our daughter, before I took him back to the VA Hospital, he asked me to take him to an address in South Los Angeles to pick up something. I stayed in my car while he went inside the house. Little did I know at that moment, he bought some drugs from a dealer. I dropped him off at the VA Hospital around 6:00 PM and went home. Little did I know it was the last time I would see him alive.

A few hours later, around 9:00 PM, I got a phone call from his mother who lived in Detroit, Michigan. She was in tears, telling me someone from the VA Hospital had called and told her that Ricky was dead. She said they told her he died from a drug overdose and that his roommate found him on the floor in the bathroom they shared. I couldn't believe what I was hearing; it felt like a nightmare, and I was going to wake up from it, and it wasn't real. Especially since I had just seen him a few hours earlier, and he was well. I couldn't believe that he was gone. I was in shock and disbelief for a long time. It was like a repeat of what happened to my first husband Gary; I just couldn't and didn't want to believe or accept it.

Losing my first and second spouses ten years apart was very difficult for me, raising my two daughters as a working single parent. I felt blessed to have my dear mother always there for me and her grandchildren. I knew I could depend on her to take care of my children while I was working long hours to pay the bills and keep a roof over our heads. Especially since she had raised eight children, including me, was a testament to everyone.

Prior to them starting preschool, I felt like she took care of my babies better than I could as a young, working mother. She loved taking care of her granddaughters. I would drop them off in the morning on my way to work and pick them up in the evening. It was a good feeling because I knew they were in good hands, getting the best care. I never had to worry about them at all, which allowed me the peace of mind to be a better person and to do a better job at work stress-free. I was able to focus on improving and expanding my business. I became better as a real estate investor, purchasing more properties, and building an impressive real estate portfolio that accumulated value in the millions of dollars in the eighties, nineties, and early thousands.

In 1987, I purchased a fourplex, which was a fixer and needed to be completely rehabbed. After the work was completely done, I moved my mother into one of the units, giving her a home to live in and not having to ever worry about a place to live in the U.S. I rented out the other three units, which brought in sufficient rent to cover the mortgage, taxes, insurance, and other expenses to maintain the property.

Through the years leading into the 20th century, I was successful in building an impressive real estate investment portfolio, ultimately creating generational wealth. Being in a financial position to provide a good life for my family meant a lot to me.

My siblings and I made sure she was well taken care of, and she never ever had to go to work at a job during the thirty-plus years she lived in this country until she passed in April 2013.

In the early nineties, while working for American Savings Bank, I reconnected with MC Collins, who later became my third husband. It happened when his Real Estate Agent, whom I had been working with as his preferred Mortgage Loan

Officer at the bank, was also working with Mr. Collins as his agent, showing him properties he was interested in buying. He brought Mr. Collins' loan application to my office for processing and approval to purchase a home he liked and was interested in buying. While reviewing his loan application, I noticed his name and other information were very familiar to me and brought back memories. I realized that he was someone I had met and dated in the mid-seventies during that time I was attending college and working with a hectic schedule and didn't have time for a committed relationship. At some point, we drifted apart, and both of us moved on, ending up with different partners. Twenty years later, we reconnected, and this time it was meant to be; we were both mature and wanted the same things in life. We fell in love and became inseparable.

MC and I married on November 25, 1999, in Las Vegas about a month and a half prior to Y2K or the 20th century, at the famous Little White Chapel, known to many as the wedding chapel where celebrities such as Michael Jordan and Joan Collins tied the knot. Many of our family members and friends traveled to Las Vegas to witness and celebrate this very special day and occasion with us.

MC was very supportive of my career and business accomplishments as a Real Estate Broker and Investor. He had been working in the Motion Pictures Entertainment Industry as a Lighting Tech. and Photographer for over twenty years.

He told me he always wanted to invest in real estate but never had the opportunity to do so because he never got the support he needed from his previous partners and always felt he was held back by different people for different reasons. He got on board right away, and we developed a partnership to start buying and investing in real estate. We were partners in life and also in real estate investments. We established a good working relationship and also became best friends along the way.

We started purchasing and rehabbing several pieces of properties, sold some, and kept some for rental income investment, creating and building generational wealth. We were able to purchase a 12-unit multifamily residential apartment building in 1996 with financing from the City of Los Angeles affordable housing program: no down payment, 100% financing, and 100% rehab financing cost. It was the best deal we were blessed to be a part of and took advantage of the program right away. I felt this was a blessing because a good friend of mine told me about the program, which was established after the 1994 Northridge earthquake by the city of LA to give small investors like us the opportunity to purchase multifamily residential properties with little to no down payment and closing cost in a market that normally required 20-25% cash down payment plus closing cost and most likely rehab cost, which would have been out of reach for small investors like us. To qualify for the special financing under the City of LA program, the multifamily property had to show damage from the devastating Northridge Earthquake on January 17, 1994, and it had to be located in the City of LA.

After living in an HOA Townhome Community for thirteen years in Inglewood, California, I decided it was time to start looking for a single-family home in a residential community. My first choice was to look for a home in my dream area, which was Ladera Heights, a community in an unincorporated area in Los Angeles County, a residential neighborhood unofficially known as the Black Beverly Hills because of the high concentration of upper-middle-class African American residents. It is known for residents of affluent African Americans. Baseball player Frank Robinson, basketball player Baron Scott, and other well-known players began moving to Ladera Heights in the early seventies. Many celebrities have moved to and lived in Ladera Heights over the years. Many of the residents include African American professionals such as doctors, lawyers, dentists, engineers, and business owners. Statistics verify that, at the end of 2020, Ladera Heights ranks #3 among the top richest black communities in the U.S., with an average family income of $132,824. The U.S. Census reported Ladera Heights had a population of 6,498. The racial makeup of Ladera Heights was 4,786 (73%) African Americans. Looking for a home in Ladera Heights took about three to four weeks to find one that was within our budget.

On August 25, 2001, I made an offer to purchase a 3-bedroom, 2-bath, 2200-square-foot house with a large backyard and a pool. The asking price of $530,000 was accepted by the seller. The kitchen and master bathroom were completely remodeled prior to moving our family to our new home on September 24, 2001, two weeks after the 9/11 terrorist attacks on the World Trade Center in New York City. We loved our new home in Ladera Heights and our new neighborhood. A few months after we moved in, I realized that our living space wasn't as large as I would like, especially the closets in our master bedroom and the other two rooms. It was a little disappointing since we had just moved from our large 3-bedroom 2 ½ baths, large walk-in closet in the master bedroom, which I had gotten used to, became a problem for us. My husband had almost no space for his clothes.

CHAPTER XIII

Building Our Dream Home

Those issues became a problem for us. After several years of dealing with this issue, we decided it was time to make plans to add on and increase the square footage in our living space.

In early 2007, we started working with my sister Sophie, an architect, and her friend David, also an architect, to start a plan to remodel our home. We had a large pool that took up a large portion of our backyard; we realized we didn't have sufficient space to increase the square feet that would make a difference in the space we wanted to add on. Our only choice was to add a second story and go up.

Working together with the Architects putting the plans together focusing on the second floor to get the required permits. They did an excellent job working with us, adding a second story included eighteen hundreds square feet, a huge master bedroom suite with large walk-in his & hers closets and large bathroom a jacuzzi tub and shower on one side. On the opposite side, two bedrooms and a Jack and Jill bathroom. The laundry room was also added on the second floor. We added a total of 1800 square feet to the original 2200 square feet, making our house a total of 4000 square feet, six bedrooms, four bathrooms, living room and dining area combine referred to as an open floor plan and a large redesigned kitchen.

It took about a year and a half from start to finish. We had to completely move out of our house for a total of six months during the construction. The house had to be completely rebuilt. The project was completed on December 15, 2007, just in time for us to move back in our new house ten days before Christmas.

On January 30, 2008, my husband, MC Collins, turned 60 years young. We decided to celebrate his big day and our new housewarming together. It was a wonderful celebration with family and friends which turned out to be the event of the year. Proudly showing off our new home and celebrating a landmark birthday sixty years for my wonderful husband. We were living the life I always dreamed of. It felt like I was on top of the world and so was he.

Rebuilding our house was a challenge and also an adventure from the beginning to the very end. From the designing stage working with the architects, my sister Sophie, and her associate architect and friend David. Working with the City of Los Angeles Department of Building and Safety to get the plans approved and building permits took almost a year to complete. Completing the first and second phases was very challenging. After that, we had to find a general contractor to begin the building process.

Finding a contractor to get cost estimates was a bigger challenge since we had no idea how much it would cost to rebuild a two-story house adding 1800 plus square feet to the original 2200 square feet, making a grand total of 4000 square feet of living space until we starting looking for general contractors and getting estimates. We were able to get estimates from 5-6 different general contractors. This process took about three to four months to accomplish.

From the beginning, we didn't realize how much it would cost to rebuild our house. We were very surprised to find out how expensive it was until we got cost estimates from 4 to 5 General Contractors prices from $400,000 up to $650,000 which was way over our budget of $350,000 to $400,000. It became a huge challenge for us.

The bids we got from the five general contractors who were from different races and ethnicity after comparing the bids we noticed that the highest bids we got was from black or African American contractors which made our decision to pick a contractor a little more difficult for us since we preferred to work with a black contractor especially because of our budget. We ultimately had to pick the contractor whose bid was closer to our budget of $400,000 and more affordable. The final cost to complete the project was $450,000 because of change orders which had to be made doing the construction.

This project turned out to be one of our biggest projects. It was worth the hard work, time, and money we put into it because we built our dream and we loved it. During the construction work, my wonderful husband, MC Collins, was at the property every day, keeping an eye on the workers to avoid delays and to meet deadlines, which was a blessing. The completion of the project was a little earlier than we had expected, saving us time and money.

Between January 30, 2008, and December 31, 2009, after we moved back to our newly rebuilt dream home, our life was everything I dreamed of. I was living my best life, not realizing how quickly things could change or take a turn for the worse.

From the crash of Wall Street leading up to the great economic recession, which officially started in the U.S. in December 2007 until June 2009. In 2008, the Democratic party nominated Barack Obama for President of the United States of America. On November 4, he defeated the Republican nominee, John McCain of Arizona, making him the President-elect, and making history as the first African American elected President of the United States of America. He also inherited the great economic recession in his first term. His administration faced the toughest challenges any newly elected president has ever experienced in modern times. Despite the many challenges and obstacles, including hate and racism as the first African American president and commander-in-chief, he and his administration saved our country from what many compared to the Great Depression. Within the first two years of his administration, a democratic Congress passed the Affordable Health Care Act for the first time in fifty years, which several administrations had failed to pass.

As a self-employed Independent Real Estate Mortgage Broker and Investor, I didn't realize how hard my business had been hit during the economic recession until about the second quarter of 2009. In early 2008, during the fall of Wall Street, the financial markets, and the real estate industry, in which I was heavily invested, I had to face the reality that the bubble had burst. This marked the beginning of my financial hardship. I had depleted my savings trying to keep my business open. Bills had to be paid but barely nothing coming in pay them just about all of the Real Estate Agents working in my office on commissions, had to leave due to lack of new business clients. Foreclosures were on the rise and people were losing their homes. Property values were declining and sinking fast. Many properties were underwater or upside down, a common expression used for referring to declining property values. Even the refinance and home equity loans business was slowing down for lack of equity or low equity value. Loan modifications were on the rise. Many people were frantically trying to save their homes by getting loan modifications. The most vulnerable were being taken advantage of by scammers. Some of whom were attorneys.

Between 2004 to 2007, we set our sights on Las Vegas, Nevada when real estate markets were booming. Within two years, we purchased six brand new houses as investments. Our plans were to rent them for a year or two, make some improvements or update them and make them more appealing to sell for profit, expecting some appreciation in the values. Surely not expecting the 2008/2009 economic recession and the devastating effect on our economy and the real estate and financial markets, which was not a part of our plans. We were blindsided and totally caught off track. The housing markets in Las Vegas were so bad, we couldn't rent or lease any of the houses for sufficient income to cover our expenses, including the mortgages. The only choice available was to put the houses up for short sale less than what it cost us because all the property value was rapidly declining and we had to sell them for less than the mortgage balance which means, we had to take a loss since we had no equity. We had to get our lender's approval to up them up for short sales.

In 2010, we came very close to losing our home just a few years after we had it completely rebuilt in 2007. It was very devastating for me because I never dreamed things would ever get that bad. I was constantly thinking of the possibility that our family could have become homeless. I kept trying to get a loan modification to save our home. Our lender, Wells Fargo Home Mortgage, kept turning us down, but I didn't give up. I kept reapplying every time they told me we didn't qualify for a modification. I was determined to save our home. It took almost two years to get a loan modification and save our home from foreclosure. If I had given up just once during those two years, the bank would have taken our home. I prayed to God every day for a miracle to save our home. I was determined not to give up and let those worthy bankers take our dream home and everything we had worked so hard for.

A year after saving my home, I almost lost my twelve-unit apartment building because of late past due property taxes on the building. The lender increased our monthly mortgage payment by two thousand dollars more than we were paying to catch up on the past due property taxes in a few months. This created a big problem for us because the monthly rental income on the building was not sufficient to cover the total operating monthly expenses. I tried to get my lender's account manager to reduce the two-thousand-dollar increase by giving us more time to pay it back in nine months instead of six months. To my surprise, he flat out refused to work with me. I flat out told him he was putting me in a position where I could lose my property. I had two vacant units I needed to rent in order to pay the additional two thousand per month.

He was a complete racist jerk who didn't give a damn about me or my situation and wanted to take my property.

After struggling for three to four months making the higher mortgage payments, I fell behind and could not make the last two monthly payments. I applied for a hard money second trust deed to save the property, but my loan application was denied by the private lender after I signed the loan documents. It was never funded. A very good friend of mine came to my rescue and loaned me the $43,000 cash needed to save my property. Once again, she was my blessing from God. I cannot thank Him enough. He's my rock and Savior. I thank God every day for waking me up and for everything I have accomplished since I came to this country with nothing but a few dollars in my pocket and have been able to survive and prosper over the years in spite of the many ups and downs he has also given me the strength to keep going and never give up.

During those difficult times, I had to make some changes to keep my business open. First, I had to cut expenses. The major step I took was to downsize my office space from twelve hundred square feet on Wilshire Boulevard, which was empty, to a smaller space of eight hundred square feet in Culver City, California, about a five-minute drive from my home in Ladera Heights. This cut my monthly office space lease cost from $2,200 per month to $1,500 per month. This move was a blessing because it saved me 60% on both my traveling time and cost.

While doing everything possible to keep my business open and relevant, I looked into other business opportunities online. I found a few hits and misses and picked up some work to keep the doors open and to survive another day. I opened an online traffic school in 2014, after completing the Department of Motor Vehicles (DMV) required approval process for a license to operate and manage an online traffic school. I felt this was going to be a great opportunity to start an online business that I could operate from the comfort of my already established office space, since I was also operating my real estate mortgage brokerage firm. I was hoping this new business would be an opportunity to earn additional income since I was still recovering from the fall of the economic recession trying to generate income from a different source.

I started this business because I learned that the online traffic school business was a new up-and-coming business in California's growing population, with an increase of over fifteen million drivers in the last few years. I was excited about this new business opportunity and strongly felt this was something I needed to do to get my finances back to where it needed to be. Unfortunately, two years after I opened the business, I had to make the hard decision to shut it down since I realized and had to admit that my online traffic school was barely breaking even and didn't see a path to making a profit any time soon. I also found out a few months after I opened my online traffic school, a lot of people had the same ideas to do what I did, many new online traffic schools open in a short time period, increasing the number of online traffic schools in a short time thus creating a high volume of competition in that space. I decided it was not a good idea to keep the business open under those circumstances. I strongly felt it was better to closed before it became a liability. I didn't see a clear path to making a profit in this business for a long time. I felt that it was time to cut my losses and move on. I decided to concentrate on my current business. I had been blessed to own and operate successfully for over fifteen years and is proudly operating it today.

Constant prayers and determination kept me going. Many of my friends and business associates used to ask me how was I able to survives the worse economic recession in this country since, the great depression and kept my business open and why didn't I close my business and get a job. I always told them I loved working for myself and I had decided that I was never going back to work in corporate America again. Although being self-employed had its challenges, I always felt that being my own boss doing what I loved for many years helping families achieve their American dreams of homeownership was my destiny.

CHAPTER XIV

Starting a Non-profit Charity Organization/T.E.N. INC

Early 2004, at the height of my successful real estate mortgage brokerage business and $12 to $15 million real estate investments portfolio, I felt it was time to give back to the most vulnerable, overlooked and underserved children and families in Africa, especially in my home country of Liberia on the West Coast of Africa. I organized and started a charitable, non-profit organization to raise much-needed funds to help educate and feed children.

On October 18, 2004, with the help of a small group of professional and business African- American women, some of whom are my sisters and close friends, The Entrepreneurial Network Inc., dba T.E.N. INC, a 501(c)3, non-profit charity/ organization was founded. My purpose for starting a charitable non-profit organization was to assist disadvantaged children in Africa. Our mission for The Entrepreneurial

Network, Inc., was to help orphan children of African descent in Africa and the U.S. Our goal is to focus on children who have lost parents and or guardians because of civil wars and ongoing conflicts in Africa, victims of extreme poverty, and HIV-AIDS in targeted communities in Africa.

Our current MISSION STATEMENT, later revised in 2016, is as follows:

> *Our mission is to assist in the welfare and care of children of African descent who live in Africa and the United States. We do this by providing financial support for basic shelter, food nourishment, and education through sponsorship and scholarship programs to help them grow up to be healthy, enlightened, and empowered.*

Rewind to my early years living in Los Angeles, close to Hollywood and in my early twenties. I was encouraged and inspired to become a high-fashion runway model. Sometimes strangers I met used to ask me if I was a model. I was five-feet, eight inches tall, one hundred and twenty pounds, in nice shape with the look of a runway model. I decided to inquire and find out how to become a model in Hollywood. I went on to interview with a few modeling agencies and was told to sign up with a modeling school to get some training. I got an interview with a professional modeling school on Sunset

Boulevard in Hollywood. At the interview, they loved me and told me that I would make a great runway high-fashion model with the proper training. They wanted to sign me up right away but the cost for the training was $600 which I had to pay before I started. The problem was I didn't have that much money and didn't know how I was going to get it. I was a struggling student, taking care of myself, just barely surviving on a tight budget. Unfortunately, that was the end of my dreams of becoming a high fashion runway model.

In 1995, I became a naturalized U.S. citizen after I passed the immigration requirements to become a U.S. citizen. I took my oath along with four thousand immigrants at the L. A. convention center in downtown Los Angeles. As a U.S. Citizen, I became eligible to vote. Before I registered to vote, I decided to do some research on the two major political parties in the country. I chose the Democratic Party for a couple of reasons. It was the Liberal Party and their policies were more aligned with my core values. It was also known as the party that recognized the majority of middle- and working-class American citizens. The very first president I voted for was Bill Clinton, in 1996, the democratic candidate for president and won. It felt good voting for the first time in exercising my civic duty.

The fact that he won made my vote even more powerful and exciting. I felt good about being able to vote and my voice was heard, and my vote was counted. I learned that back in the fifties and sixties many Blacks or Africa Americans were denied their freedom and rights to vote. Many had to and died for their civic rights to vote. Having the freedom and opportunity to exercise my right to vote was a major step for me as a citizen in the U.S. At first, I didn't care to get involved in politics except to exercise my constitutional right to vote for president. Until Barack Obama announced his decision to run for president in 2007 to become the first Africa American in the history of this country. I did my research on him and found out that he was highly educated and qualified for the job. I decided to join his campaign and became a volunteer. I also joined the local democratic club in the 47th Assembly District where I lived, became a grassroot activist and worked to support his campaign. I was motivated and excited about Barack's candidacy and the possibility of him winning and becoming the first African American President and Commander-in-Chief.

I started talking to my family members and friends about Barack Obama and trying to encourage them to consider voting for him not only because he was black- Africa American but also because he was a highly educated president of Harvard law review and highly qualified. Going door-to-door canvassing in my neighborhood and phone banking, calling democrats all over the country, encouraging them to vote for Barack Obama, reminding them of his agenda. I work with his national campaign office fundraising team in Chicago, IL.

I also hosted several fundraising and phone banking events at my home in Los Angeles and was able to raise a few thousand dollars from small donors for his campaign. My strong support for Barack Obama was unwavering. I took action early on as a supporter in his campaign because I felt that he was qualified to become the first African American president of the U.S. A. and wanted to do my part to ensure his victory and history. I felt it was important to put my money where my mouth was and do what I could to achieve victory for his campaign and alternately for the American people.

As an African who came to this country as an immigrant and became a naturalized citizen, I felt a strong connection to Barack because of his father who was born in Kenya, East Africa. I read his book Dreams From My Father which told the story of his father and his family in Kenya.

On election day November 2007 after all the votes were counted, and the winner was announced, I was very happy we won and celebrated all night with fellow Dems. Supporters at the Century Plaza Hotel in Century City. It was amazing to be a part of and a witness to this historic event in my lifetime. I traveled to Washington DC on January 20, 2008, for the first time, to witness the inauguration ceremony for President Obama. Which turned out to be the largest crowd ever in attendance at any presidential inauguration ceremony in history at the Washington Mall.

It was very exciting to witness the first elected African American President take his oath to officially become

President of the United States of America. This motivated me even more to get involved in America's political system after President Obama took office. I made a conscious decision to follow and support his presidency for the entire eight years of his administration.

January 20, 2009, I decided to run for a Delegate position in the 47th Assembly District and won with six other candidates for the California State Democratic Party.

During his first two years in office, President Obama and his Democratic allies in Congress compiled a substantial record of policy accomplishments. His first action addressed the global financial crisis and included a major stimulus package bringing our financial systems from the brink of collapse. Rescuing two American automakers, passing the Affordable Care Act into law, sweeping reform of financial regulations and major changes in student loan programs.

Nevertheless, the political standing of both the president and Congressional Democrats slipped steadily through much of this period and voters administered a substantial rebuke in the November 2010 midterms elections.

In spite of the Republicans' plans from day one to make President Obama a one term president failed. He was re-elected for a second term in 2012. Even though, they controlled Congress for six of his eight years of administration and made it very difficult for him to get many of his policies through Congress. Despise his efforts to reach across the aisles to create bipartisanship with both parties. Most of his agendas were stalled or blocked by republicans in Congress.

Fast forward to 2017 when I experienced yet another discrimination. It happened after I applied for a million loan to refinance my 12-unit multifamily residential apartment building located in the heart of the African American community in the Baldwin Vista area, City of Los Angeles. This was something I was not expecting and will never forget it hit me so hard that I almost lost my property. I had to refinance my property because I had to pay off a first and second trust deed loans which were both about to mature and balloon payments had to be payoff in six months or sooner. I did some checking for and found a lender, Sun West Mortgage, with the financing program I needed within a small commercial residential loan starting from one million up to $3.5 million to be underwritten, approved and funded by the Federal National Mortgage Corporation/Freddie Mac, one of the largest secondary mortgage servicer in the U.S. My application had to be originated by Sun West Mortgage a wholesales lender in the primary mortgage lending market, under Freddie Mac's guidelines in order to be underwritten, approve and fund by them.

My current five-year fixed-rate mortgage was about to mature in six months with a balloon payment of approximately $550,000 plus a $100,000 private money second T.D. to payoff. I started the loan application process six months prior to the maturity date in order to close on time. I was very careful in following their pre-approval guidelines before submitting my loan application because I was concerned about their $10,000 up front nonrefundable application fee to cover the loan processing such as appraisal, inspection and legal fees. Which I had some concern about losing in case my loan application didn't get approved. After my loan application was processed and submitted to Freddie Mac for approval and funding.

About a week after my application package was submitted, I got a call from my Sun West Mortgage Account Executive, telling me that Freddie Mac's underwriter had denied my loan application. I was shocked because I was expecting an approval since we were sure that I had met and satisfied all their guidelines and requirements for the loan program.

It took a few days before I was able to speak with a Freddie Mac underwriting manager and ask for a letter of adverse action, which is required by law to inform the borrower in writing of the reasons the loan was denied. To my surprise, they told me my loan was denied because they didn't or couldn't verify sufficient cash or liquid assets in my bank accounts. This was a surprise to me because during the processing of my loan application, no one, not even my account executive, told me they needed to verify a certain amount of cash or liquid assets in my accounts. This information was also not mentioned in their pre-approval requirements. I was very upset that my loan was denied for something that I was unaware of at the beginning or during the processing of my loan. To add insult to injury, I requested a refund of the $10,000 application fee I had to give them before my loan application was accepted. I was shocked when they told me that after the fees were added up, the total processing fees exceeded the $10,000 deposit I had given them, and I owed them a balance of approximately $2,500. I had to pay the balance to them before they would release a copy of the appraisal, which cost $3,500, and which I needed to take to another lender for a loan. Those individuals denied my loan application for no good reason, spent my $10,000, and had the nerve to demand that I pay them an additional $2,500 before I could get the original appraisal I had already paid for. I was very upset and thought I had an attorney who would represent me and sue them for discrimination in real estate financing, but a month or so after the incident, the attorney I was depending on to take this big corporation to court backed out without giving me any reason and returned the retainer fee.

I had a difficult time trying to find another attorney to replace him. At that time, I was about a month away from my current loan maturity date and still had to get a new lender to refinance my property before my loan went into default and put my property at risk of foreclosure, which came very close. The pressure was on, and I was running out of time to save my property from foreclosure. Fortunately for me, with some connections and referrals, I was able to find another lender just in time to get a million dollars loan approved to refinance and save my property.

Going through this process, I realized this was another typical case of redlining and discrimination in real estate financing. I decided to sue Sun West Mortgage and Freddie Mac for real estate redlining and discrimination. Unfortunately for me, the lawyer who I thought was a friend and had promised to represent me in this case had a change of mind several months later and decided not to take my case to court, giving me no reason for his decision. It was clear that he was unwilling to take on a big corporation and a powerful lender like Freddie Mac unless he could build a class action lawsuit against them. I made several attempts to find another lawyer to take my case but was unsuccessful. I was very disappointed and frustrated that I couldn't find a civil rights lawyer to represent me against a big white own corporation own got away. I decided to move on.

CHAPTER XV

My Firt Trip Back Home in 1973

In the summer of 1973 after four years of living in the U.S., working, and attending college, I felt that it was time to take a break or a vacation and go back home for a few weeks. Most of my family including my mother, Grandma, and five of my siblings were still living in Liberia. I felt it was time for a break and looking forward to going back home for the first time after 4 years to see my family and friends who I love and miss so much.

I bought a round-trip ticket and took a flight from Los Angeles Intl. Airport (LAX) to J.F.K. International Airport (NYC) transferred to another flight to Roberts Field Intl. Airport Monrovia, Liberia making one stop in Dakar, Senegal, and arriving about 24 hours later the next day. I was very happy and excited and excited to arrive in Liberia on a long trip back home. My Mom prepared one of my favorite Liberian dishes, Palava sauce, and futu. It was very testy and spices.

I couldn't stop eating until my bow was empty. Being back home for my first visit in 4 years was an experience I just couldn't translate into words. Except it felt like two completely different worlds coming together from a huge country U.S.A. to a small country Liberia was like putting a big and a small puzzle together at the same time.

Spending time at home with my family and friends after being in the States felt like healing for my mind body and soul and was exactly what the doctor ordered. One of the best parts of being back home was eating and enjoying authentic Liberian food like Cassava Leaves, Jollif Rice, Potatoes Greens, Collard Greens, Pepper Soup, and Fufu & Palava Sauce every day was like being in heaven. All of these are plant-based food grown organically and locally in Liberia. No added chemicals such as pesticides. The food was always fresh and delicious. It was very difficult to leave after, being spoiled by my family, especially my mom cooking every day.

CHAPTER XVI

Becoming a Grandmother

Becoming a grandmother for the first time was one of the most rewarding experiences of my life. On November 14, 2003, my first daughter, Gwendolyn II, gave birth to her first child, and my first granddaughter, a precious baby girl named Daiya Devine. I remember the first time I held her in my arms; my heart melted, filled with an abundance of love for this precious gift from God. That moment transported me back to the day I gave birth to my first child on December 28, 1980, just three days after Christmas—the best gift I could have ever imagined from the Lord. I felt blessed beyond measure; she stole my heart.

About a year and a half later, on August 1, 2005, my daughter gave birth to her second daughter, another precious angel and gift from God named Hasana Medina Drew, my second granddaughter, who also completely stole my heart. Since I didn't feel or look like a grandmother, I asked them to call me Nana instead of Grandma.

In September 2013, a few months after losing my dearest mother and still grieving her loss, my daughter Gwendolyn II, nicknamed Tricia, informed me she was tired of Los Angeles and was moving to Miami, Florida, taking her kids, my granddaughters, 2,733 miles away from me. They were only eight and ten years old. I was devastated because I didn't want my daughter and grandkids living so far away from me in another state. I wanted to be in their lives and watch them grow up. I didn't want to wake up one day and realize that they had grown up and didn't really know their grandmother, and I had missed out on their early growth.

Since I couldn't convince my daughter to stay, I paid for their round-trip tickets to come to Los Angeles to spend every summer vacation with me until they finished high school. I kept my word and did exactly what I said until my oldest granddaughter, Hadaiya, graduated from high school in May 2021 in Atlanta, Georgia. They had moved to Atlanta from Miami three years after moving to Miami because living there wasn't as they had anticipated. My second granddaughter, Hasana, graduated from high school in May of 2023, and I attended her graduation in Atlanta.

CHAPTER XVII

Our Las Vegas Wedding

Flashback to November 25, 1999, to our wedding in Las Vegas, Nevada. MC Collins, my third husband, and I tied the knot at the famous Little White Chapel on the Las Vegas Strip, renowned for being the chapel of choice for celebrities such as Michael Jordan, Joan Collins, Britney Spears, Bruce Willis, and Demi Moore, among others. Many of our family and friends had come to Las Vegas to witness the ceremony and to celebrate and share this very special occasion with us.

Before the ceremony, on Saturday, MC arranged for a limousine to transport me and my bridesmaids—my two daughters, Tricia and Erica, and my longtime best friend, Violet Thomas—from Los Angeles to Las Vegas, making it a dream trip for us. We had a blast in the limo, sipping champagne, listening to music, laughing, and chatting.

We rented a penthouse suite at the renowned Mirage Las Vegas Hotel & Casino on the Las Vegas Strip, where we had the reception and party. There were champagne toasts for the bride and groom, plenty of food, and great R&B music. My big brother, James, traveled all the way from Philadelphia, Pennsylvania, to stand in for my father and give me away. It was one of the best times of my life, and I didn't want the night to end.

A few days later, we embarked on our honeymoon to Hawaii, and it turned out to be one of the best trips ever for both of us.

CHAPTER XVIII

Second Trip to Liberia in April 2018

On April 15, 2018, I embarked on my second trip to Liberia, forty-five years after my initial visit in 1973. This time, my sister Sophie accompanied me, making it a much better experience than traveling alone on the lengthy journey from Los Angeles, California, to Liberia, West Africa.

The reason for the long delay in returning home was the tumultuous situation in our country, particularly the coup d'état in 1978, the year I had planned to make my second trip. President William R. Tolbert and many government officials were assassinated, leading to the overthrow of the Liberian government by a group of illiterate military soldiers. Subsequently, a civil war erupted, lasting approximately seventeen to eighteen long years. I had to cancel my travel plans, as it was impossible to return home amid such violent turmoil. Originally, I had intended to take some time off after graduating froMCollege with a B.A. in Business

Administration, specializing in finance management, and explore the possibility of opening a bank in Monrovia, Liberia, owned and operated by Liberians. Sadly, these plans had to be put on hold indefinitely.

We arrived in Monrovia, Liberia, at Robert Field International Airport on Easter Sunday at 7:00 p.m. local time after twenty-four long hours of travel. Despite feeling excited and exhausted, we were grateful to have arrived safely home by the grace of God. It was a wonderful feeling to be back, and Sophie and I were overjoyed to reconnect with many family members and friends we hadn't seen in years.

The changes in our country since our childhood in the fifties and sixties were striking; it was almost unrecognizable. The once beautiful city where we grew up had transformed, especially after enduring a coup d'état and two bloody civil wars in a small country plagued by suffering and poverty. It was disheartening to learn that these wars had claimed the lives of over two hundred and fifty thousand Liberian people within twenty years. I felt profound sadness and disappointment about the loss of innocent lives and the destruction of countless properties, compounded by the lack of meaningful efforts from government officials or leaders to rebuild the country and improve the lives of the Liberian people.

During our return trip to the U.S., we had planned a two-day stop in Barcelona, Spain, a beautiful city I had always wanted to visit. However, because of a missed connecting flight from Brussels to Barcelona, we experienced a twelve-hour delay at the airport before catching another flight. We arrived in Barcelona late at night and quickly checked into our Airbnb, taking a shower and getting some rest to prepare for our only full day in the city. The next day, we embarked on a day-long bus tour of Barcelona, making stops at popular tourist areas downtown and beaches, where we could hop on and off the bus tour at our leisure until completing the full tour. Despite the short duration, we took many pictures and had a wonderful time exploring Barcelona, hoping to return for a longer visit in the future.

Our two-week trip to West Africa and Europe concluded on a high note as we safely returned home, grateful for the experiences and memories created along the way, guided by the grace of God.

CHAPTER XIX

Third Trip Back Home in 2019

About a year and a half after my second trip to Liberia in April 2018, I decided to take a third trip to West Africa, Liberia, and Accra, Ghana. This time with my younger daughter Erica and her friend Jamie. The first trip to Africa was for both of them.

We flew on a Delta Airlines 9-10 flight nonstop from Los Angeles to London, England; we spent two days in London, took Air Portugal from London to Lisbon, Portugal, stayed one night in Lisbon then off to Accra, Ghana for a four-day stay.

This being our first trip to Ghana, we visited several historic sites, including the Last Door or The Door of No Return at Cape Cobb. The port where many Africans were captured and forced to leave their countries, bound and forced into slavery put on terrible ships where they were changed and packed like sardines in horrible conditions bringing them to this country.

We paid for and took a guided tour of the place and learned about the horror and torture of our ancestors and how they were taken and forced into slavery. What we learned and saw doing the tour was very difficult and heartbreaking for me, especially in the dungeon where they held for hours and days standing up very close together, with no clothes and very little to no air coming through a tiny hole at the top of the dungeon. I couldn't control my emotions tearing up at times thinking about the horror and suffering they had to endure many of them did not survive. I refused to go to a second one where they kept the women who were underground where I knew it was it would have been worse than the first one.

The next day we took a visit to the Black Star Stadium, Kwame Nkrumah stature, Museum, and grave site. The late Prime Minister of Ghana was very instrumental in achieving Ghana's independence in 1957. Kwame Nkrumah, of the Convention People's Party (CPP) became the Prime Minister of Ghana on March 6, 1957, led by the Big Six. The Gold Coast declared independence from the British and was named Ghana.

We also took a tour of Jamestown, a community that emerged around the 17th Century with Accra as the city grew. We did some shopping at one of the local marketing places and purchased some beautiful African clothing, arts, and accessories to support the local African merchants.

We had a wonderful short four-day vacation in Ghana. The people we met were very nice.

Our next and last stop was Monrovia, Liberia, back home for me, the first visit for Erica and Jamie. They had a short four-day stay in Liberia because they had a total of two weeks' vacation. I stayed ten days in Liberia because I am self-employed and am the boss. We stayed at my cousin Rhonda and her family's guest house which was very nice and cozy. She also let us use one of the cars and a driver for as long as we were in Liberia. The first day we took a tour of Monrovia, the Capital City. The next day we spent at Mabassa, a beautiful vacation resort on a private beach with a restaurant that serves authentic Liberian, and West African food, very nice private lodging Bungalows. Tourists enjoy a walk on the clean, private beach and relax all day. We had a wonderful day out there with family and friends.

The third day I took my daughter to see the high school I graduated from, St Teresa's Convent, a catholic school for girls. We also got invites to dinner by family members we hadn't seen in a long time and enjoyed more delicious Liberian food.

After Erica and Jamie left for home, I spent the rest of my vacation with family and friends and had a wonderful vacation. I returned home alone on November 26, 2019. It was nice to be home and get some rest after traveling so far from home for so long.

THE
CAPITAL
ROOM
EST. MMXV

Liberia with Erica and Jamie

Liberia at St Teresa's Convent with students

Erica at St. Teresa's Convent

With Teacher at St. Teresa's Convent

Me and Erica at St. Teresa's Convent campus

Gwendolyn P. Cassell Austin-Collins

A beach in Monrovia, Liberia

CLOSING

When I decided to tell my story during the lockdown in December 2020, I wanted to tell my readers about me, the real person. Starting with my hobbies, what I love and enjoy doing, and some of my beliefs.

I love people, especially my family and friends. I prefer love over hate, any day even on my worst days.

I am not a perfect human being and never claim to be.

I believe there are no perfect human beings on this earth. All humans have false beliefs. The only exception is: our Lord and Savior Jesus Christ, the only Begotten son of our Heavenly Father who was crucified, died, and buried and had risen from the dead on the third day, Easter Sunday.

I believe there's only one race: THE HUMAN RACE.

I believe no human race should be identified by the color of their skin.

The simple fact is every human being on this earth has the same color of red blood in their veins. No matter who you are where you come from or the "so-called" color of your skin.

FACTS: The skin is a pigmentation and the largest organ of the human body and covers the

Entire body. Using the color of the skin to identify our race is just wrong.

The color of our skin does not identify our race. This is a myth or misconception that has

been rooted in society by a certain group of people who decided to identify the human race using skin color to divide and separate the human race by the skin to discriminating against dark skin people who originated from the continent of Africa, the second largest continent in the world.

And also, to portray themselves as the superior race because of their lighter skin.

MY HOBBIES

MUSIC: My love for music has always been at the top of my list and plays a major part in my life. From a young age, I have loved the sound of music, the rhythm and blues.

Some of my favorite music is: highlife originated in West Africa, afrobeat, jazz, soul, R&B, gospel, Caribbean, and reggae. I listen to music every day from the moment I wake up in the morning, I turn on the radio and listen to The Steve Harvey Morning Show on KJLH, my favorite radio station in LA, owned by the great one and only, Stevie Wonder. I also listen to them on my way to and from work. Listening to KJLH is where I get the latest news, what's going on in the community, and some comedy which always makes me laugh, lifts my spirit, starts my day, and takes me to a better place.

DANCING: Listening to music every day makes me want to dance and become one of my favorite social pastimes. As a little girl growing up in Liberia, I enjoyed watching my parents and other grown people dance. My Mom who loved to dance, inspired me to want to dance like her. I always remember back in the day, one of her favorite dances was the Cha, Cha. In high school, my desire to dance became an obsession.

I wanted to attend all the school social events where music was always playing and I was always on the dance floor having the time of my life with my friends. My love for dancing was and is still rooted in my DNA. It got me in trouble with my father a few times. When I did something that I knew I wasn't supposed to do, my punishment was that I couldn't go to a school social event. I had planned to attend and all my classmates and friends were expecting me. It hurt so bad I felt like he had put a knife in my heart. Being disobedient sometimes, I decided that I was going to this particular event because it was one of the biggest events and I wasn't going to miss it for any cause. After my parents went to bed, I decided to sneak out with my oldest brother James, who took me to the event. I got caught that night by my father, who woke up before the event was over, and found out that I wasn't in my bed sleeping and decided to come get me. I was so embarrassed I wished the floor could have opened and swallowed me up.

CONCERTS: Another one of my favorite pastimes is going to concerts with my husband. We enjoy going to music concerts in the late eighties and nineties, to see our favorite artists to name a few: Earth, Wind & Fire, Frankie Beverly and Maze, Luther Vandross, Anita Baker, Arthea Franklin, Tina Turner, Stevie Wonder, The Temptation, Toni Braxton, Michael Jackson, Sade, and the list goes.

COMEDY: I love to laugh and going to see a comedy show, has become one of my favorite pastimes. We love going to the Laugh Factory on Sunset Blvd and other comedy clubs every time we could on the weekend. I enjoy watching comedy movies and TV shows which always make me laugh and lift my spirits. Some of my favorite comedians are #1 Richard Pryor, who I met at a popular Speak Easy Night Club on Santa Monica Blvd. in Hollywood, and Eddie Murphy, who I saw up close on Wilshire Blvd across the street from my office building while shooting a scene for Beverly Hills Cobs. Chris Rock, Red Foxx, Martin Lawrence Jamie Fox, and many more.

TRAVELING: I love to travel, which became a passion for me. My love for traveling started when I came to America in the early seventies, in my twenties.

Being the first in my family to move to Los Angeles, California, in the early seventies, with most of my family living in different States on the East Coast, I started traveling to New York, Philadelphia, Maryland to visit My big brother, James who lived in Philly, other siblings, and family members living on the East Coast.

The fact that I was an immigrant from a small country so far away who came to this huge country was very exciting to me and to realize that I could travel to all these different cities and states to see people I love was amazing. My love and passion for traveling took on a new chapel in my life. Later, after I got married, became a U.S. Citizen, and got a U. S. passport to travel out of the country, I embarked on an international travel adventure.

I traveled to several countries in Europe, and Africa, several cruises to the Caribbean Islands, The Virgin Islands, the Mexican Riviera, Cancun, and Jamaica. After I became a wife and mother of two beautiful daughters, I started taking both of them with me on vacation, usually during the summer every year. We always travel to a city or states on the East Coast like New York, Philadelphia, Maryland, and the Midwest like Michigan, Chicago, and Ohio to meet and visit family members on both sides. We all had lots of fun visiting and meeting family members, especially connecting with the younger ones in their age group.

My younger daughter, Erica, loves to travel like me after she was bitten by the travel bug early on her first trip at the young age of nine months old to Atlanta, GA.

THE MOVIES: I love going to the movies. Growing up in Libera, I discovered my love for movies in my early teens. Going to the theater on the weekend every chance I got to see a movie with friends became a passion and favorite pastime for me.

Even after I came to America to attend college, I continued to go to the movies for entertainment and also as one of my favorite times to relax. When I met my first husband Gary, who enjoyed going to the movies as much as I did, together it became our favorite pastime. I remember going to see the first Star Wars movie on Hollywood Boulevard, standing in long lines for a few hours to get our tickets, I was pregnant with our first child.

Throughout my lifetime, going to the movies with my family and friends has been important in my life then and now. Taking my children to the theater to see and enjoy movies made for kids on the weekends, as a parent, meant a lot to me. I enjoy watching the movies just as much as they did.

READING: Reading is and has always been one of my favorite things. From an early age, as a little girl growing up in Liberia, I discovered and developed a passion for reading. Starting with learning to read kid books in kindergarten and elementary school, as I got to junior and senior high school, my love for reading grew stronger.

I strongly feel that my passion for reading came from my father, who was an avid reader. He taught me a lot about life and the world which he learned from every book or magazine he could get his hands on. Reading was surely one of his passions. He told me he read a book or two to three magazines in one night.

As a teenager, I used to love reading romantic magazines such as *True Confession*. My father used to encourage me to read magazines such as *Time, Life, Newsweek,* and *Ebony,* which he felt would be better and more practical to improve my overall knowledge in reading and learning. I miss him very much. He took his last breath, while reading one of his favorite books at night, in his bed next to my mother, when he suffered a heart attack at the young age of 52 during my last year of high school. It took me a long time to accept his passing, especially since he wasn't sick. It was a total shock to our family. I felt extremely sad that he was not present on my graduation day a few months after his passing.

Looking back at my life, I give full credit to my father and mother for who I am and what I have accomplished in my life today. They taught me many life lessons, to be proud of myself and of who I am, to get a good education because nobody can ever take it away from me and to dream big, I can be who and whatever I want to be, to always be ready and able to take care of myself not to depend on anybody to take care of me and to always love myself, my family, and to love others.

Looking back in the rearview mirror, at some of my life experiences, I would like to share one which I feel will be important to my readers.

After graduating from Pacific States University, Magna Cum Laude with a BA Degree in Business Administration, Finance & International Marketing major while working at Wells Fargo Bank. I decided it was time to advance my career in Banking. I inquired and applied for a position in the bank's management training program. I learned that as an employee I had to request a letter of recommendation from my supervisor and the branch manager Which I did and to my surprise they refused to write the letter on my behalf to the elite training program. According to them, I wasn't good enough or smart enough to get their Recommendation because of the color of my skin. They couldn't say that I wasn't qualified or didn't have the credentials, because I did and felt that I was more qualified than many of the other candidates. This was happening in the mid-1970s during a time when African American women were grossly overlooked and underrepresented in banking and corporate America. I wasn't surprised or naïve about discrimination in this country. It made me more determined to fight for what I considered to be my dream job at that time. I had to fight with every tool I had to get the job done, which I did. After all was said and done, I eventually got offered a position in the elite management, training program despite their efforts to stop me. I never gave up because my determination was stronger and I claimed the position. I successfully completed a one-year on-the-job training program and was offered a position as a Branch Consumer Loan Officer which I held for five years and moved on to a higher management position at Bank of America.

I wanted to mention this experience to encourage my readers especially my young readers to never give up on yourself and to never let anybody tell you that you can't when you believe in yourself that you can.

Moving forward I decided to share some meaningful advice and quotes that I felt helped guide me through a successful career path and many lessons learned.

"The only difference between success and failure is the ability to take action." –Alexander Graham Bell

"You need to make a commitment and once you make it, then life will give you some Answer." –Les Brown

"Failure is a learning experience and the guy who never failed has never done anything." –Wilson Gretbatch

"Don't wait for someone else to make your life terrific, that's your job."

"No life ever grows great until it is focused, dedicated, and disciplined."

"It's when things get rough, and you don't quit that's when success comes."

"Daily action brings results and success later."

"There's no scarcity of opportunity to make a living at what you love. There is only a scarcity of resolve to make it happen." –Wayne Dyer

"The success combination in business is: Do what you do better and more of what you do." –David Joseph Schwartz

"You don't have to be great to get started but you have to get started to be great."

"Nothing worthwhile comes easily work, continuous work and hard work is the only way to accomplish results that lasts." – Hamilton Holt

"*Learn something new, try something different. Convince yourself that you have no limits.*" – Brain Tracy

"*The most essential factor is persistence the determination never to allow your energy or enthusiasm to be dampened by discouragement that must inevitably come.*" –James Whilcomb Riley

"*We must give more in order to get more. It is the generous giving of ourselves that produces the generous harvest.*" –Orison Swett Mardon

"*Only you can hold yourself back, only you can stand in your own way, only you can help yourself.*" –Mikhail Strabo

"*Don't be afraid to fail, don't waste energy trying to cover up failure. Learn from your failures and go on to the next challenge. It's okay to fail. If you're not failing you're not growing.*" –Stanley Judd

"*Success seems to be connected with action successful men keep moving they make mistakes but they don't quit.*"

"*What you choose to focus your mind on is critical because you will become what you think about most of the time.*"

Before I end this book, I would like to include what I feel is a very powerful quote by Denzel Washington which, I would also like to share with my readers. It goes like this:

"Dreams without goals are just dreams and ultimately, they fuel disappointment. On the road to achieving your dreams, you must apply discipline but more importantly consistency because without commitment you will never start but, without consistency you will never finish."

My Family

My oldest brother, James, and me.

Me, Erica, and MC

Liberia with my Mother and two sisters, Mai and Sophrinia

My 2 daughters Gwendolyn II and Erica

My father and big brother, James Sr. and James Jr.